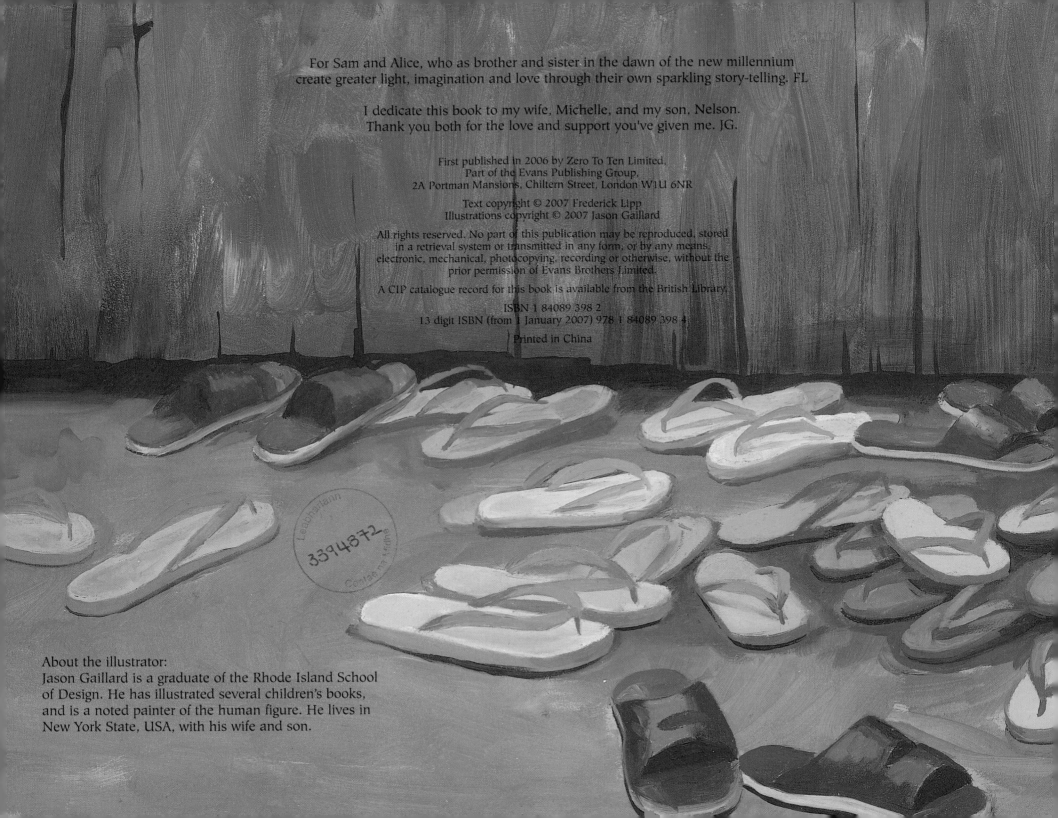

For Sam and Alice, who as brother and sister in the dawn of the new millennium
create greater light, imagination and love through their own sparkling story-telling. FL

I dedicate this book to my wife, Michelle, and my son, Nelson.
Thank you both for the love and support you've given me. JG.

First published in 2006 by Zero To Ten Limited,
Part of the Evans Publishing Group,
2A Portman Mansions, Chiltern Street, London W1U 6NR

Text copyright © 2007 Frederick Lipp
Illustrations copyright © 2007 Jason Gaillard

A CIP catalogue record for this book is available from the British Library.

ISBN 1 84089 398 2
13 digit ISBN (from 1 January 2007) 978 1 84089 398 4
Printed in China

About the illustrator:
Jason Gaillard is a graduate of the Rhode Island School
of Design. He has illustrated several children's books,
and is a noted painter of the human figure. He lives in
New York State, USA, with his wife and son.

Running Shoes

by Frederick Lipp

illustrated by Jason Gaillard

Frederick Lipp is an award winning author of children's books and the founder and president of the Cambodian Arts and Scholarship Foundation, a body that provides funding and education for impoverished children in Cambodia. Frederick lives in Maine, USA, with his wife Kitty.

Sophy lived in a land where it was nearly always hot and sunny.
And when it finally rained, it rained for days and nights without end.

One terribly hot day, Sophy squinted her eyes against the blinding sun.

The air was still. Suddenly a noise like bees swarming from a tree grew louder
and louder. The pig began snorting. The chickens cackled.

Sophy sat up straight like a bamboo shoot.

Must be the number man's jeep, she thought, as she rubbed her eyes.

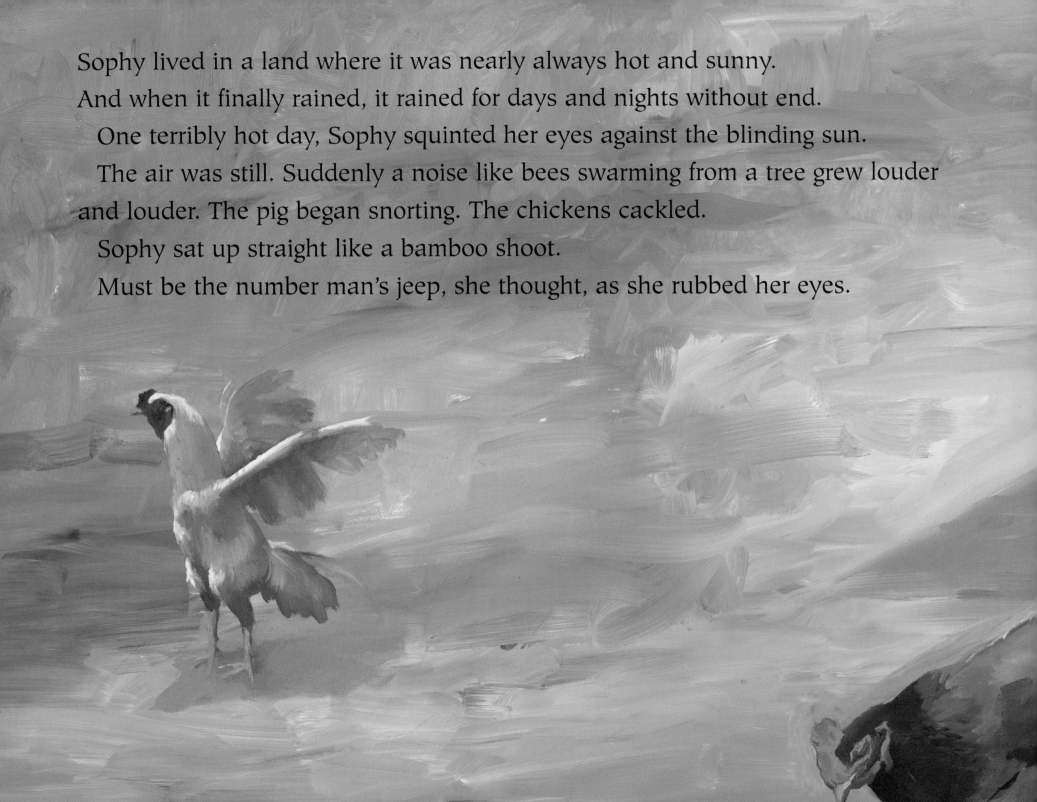

Once a year a man came from the city in a red jeep. The village people called him the number man. The number man counted the number of people in the village for the government. After making the rounds, the number man stopped at Sophy's house.

"How many people live here?" he asked.

"Two" Sophy answered. "My mother and I."

"Let's see, that comes to one hundred fifty-four people in the village. Last year there were..." The number man stopped. He'd heard in the village that Sophy's father died because there was no doctor or hospital near the village.

Sophy stared at the man's shoes.

"Ah, you have never seen running shoes before?"

Sophy blushed. She thought about her secret wish. Her wish felt far, far away like a hawk lazily soaring in circles upward in a blue sky. Deep in her heart she knew if she had a pair of shoes like the number man, her wish would come true.

"Walk with me to the side of the river," the number man said.

"Stick your feet into the soft clay… now step out." Sophy liked the warm feeling of mud squishing between her toes.

The number man took a stick from his pocket with lots of numbers. He measured Sophy's footprints.

Then the number man rubbed his chin as he mumbled numbers to himself. "Let's see… after thirty nights, you will receive a surprise."

Sophy counted the nights until a post van drove through the village, dropping off a package by her door. She held her breath as she tore open the package. "Running shoes," Sophy yelled.

She carefully put on each shoe. "Now my wish will come true,"

"What wish?" her mother asked.

"Mother, I wish to go to school."

"But the school is eight kilometres away over horrible roads."

"Yes, but now I have running shoes," Sophy said, as she bounced up and down.

A smile slowly came over Sophy's mother's face. She remembered how Sophy's father took out a small blackboard the size of a lotus leaf. Under the shade of a coconut tree, he wrote Sophy a few marks on the blackboard he called words. "This mark is your name and this is the name of our village," he taught her.

"You may go to school," Sophy's mother said.

The next day before the sun rose, Sophy ate a bowl of rice and a little salt fish. Then she set off through the rice fields, running.

The shoes protected her feet from the sharp red rocks. She sailed through the air the way a small flat stone skips over water.

She jumped over little streams and ran over a road through the jungle where only one car a month passed. Sophy ran faster and faster until finally she saw the one-room schoolhouse.

Children's sandals were lined up outside the door. Sophy hurriedly untied her running shoes, placed them by the door and walked barefoot into the schoolroom.

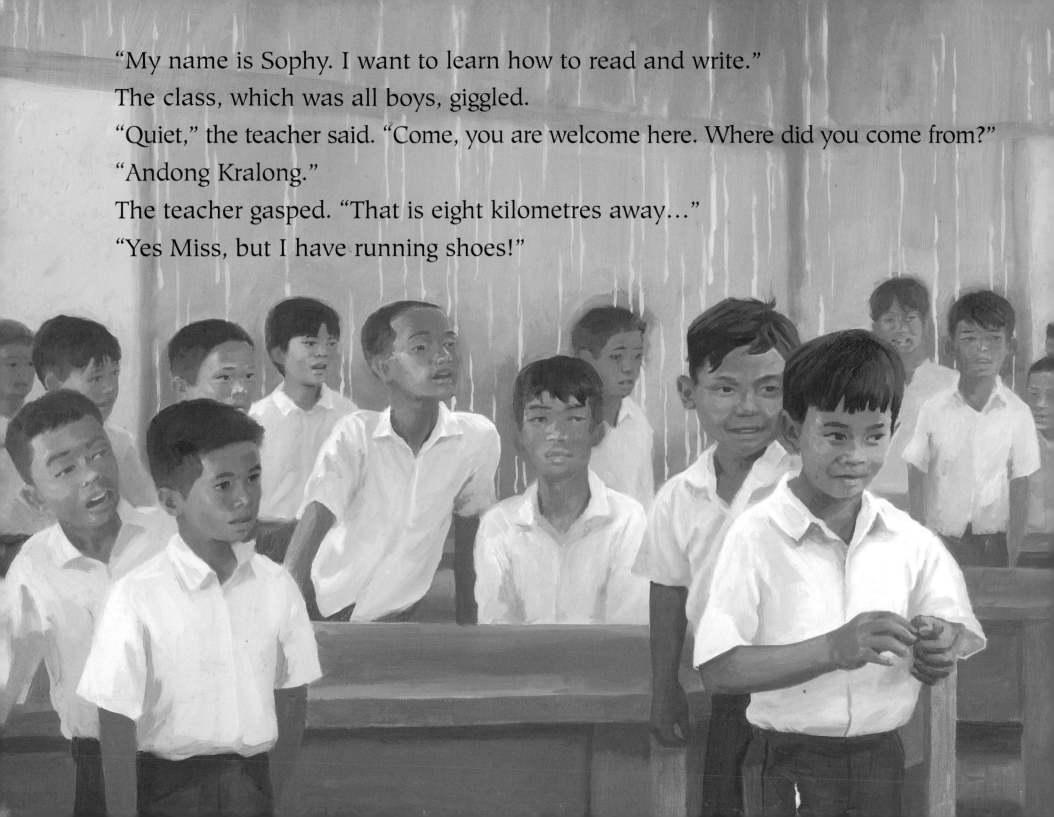

"My name is Sophy. I want to learn how to read and write."

The class, which was all boys, giggled.

"Quiet," the teacher said. "Come, you are welcome here. Where did you come from?"

"Andong Kralong."

The teacher gasped. "That is eight kilometres away..."

"Yes Miss, but I have running shoes!"

The boys covered their teeth as they laughed. Little tears
ran from Sophy's eyes. "I want to learn how to read."
"But, you're a girl," one boy whispered.
Sophy pulled all her courage together like a green snake
ready to strike. She waited for the right time to speak.

After school Sophy tied on her running shoes with three knots in each shoe. She looked over the boys and said, "If you think you are so smart, then try to catch me."

Boys pushed and shoved each other out of the way.

They ran after Sophy.

The following morning, Sophy woke before the cockerel's first call. Her head start allowed her to arrive at school before there were any sandals lined up at the door. When the boys paraded into the classroom, they smiled shyly.

They remembered how Sophy won the race.

From that day Sophy learned many subjects taught at the one-room schoolhouse.

One morning, a year later, Sophy sat with her mother
as a cloud of dust suddenly rose over the hill.
The pig began snorting. The chickens cackled.
It was the number man coming in his red jeep.
In that moment the first sprinkle of rain made little circles grow ever larger
in the river. Monsoon was beginning. Sophy looked up at the gathering
clouds and thought she would be cooler in her daily race to school.

The number man counted everyone in the village.
At the end of the day he arrived at Sophy's house.

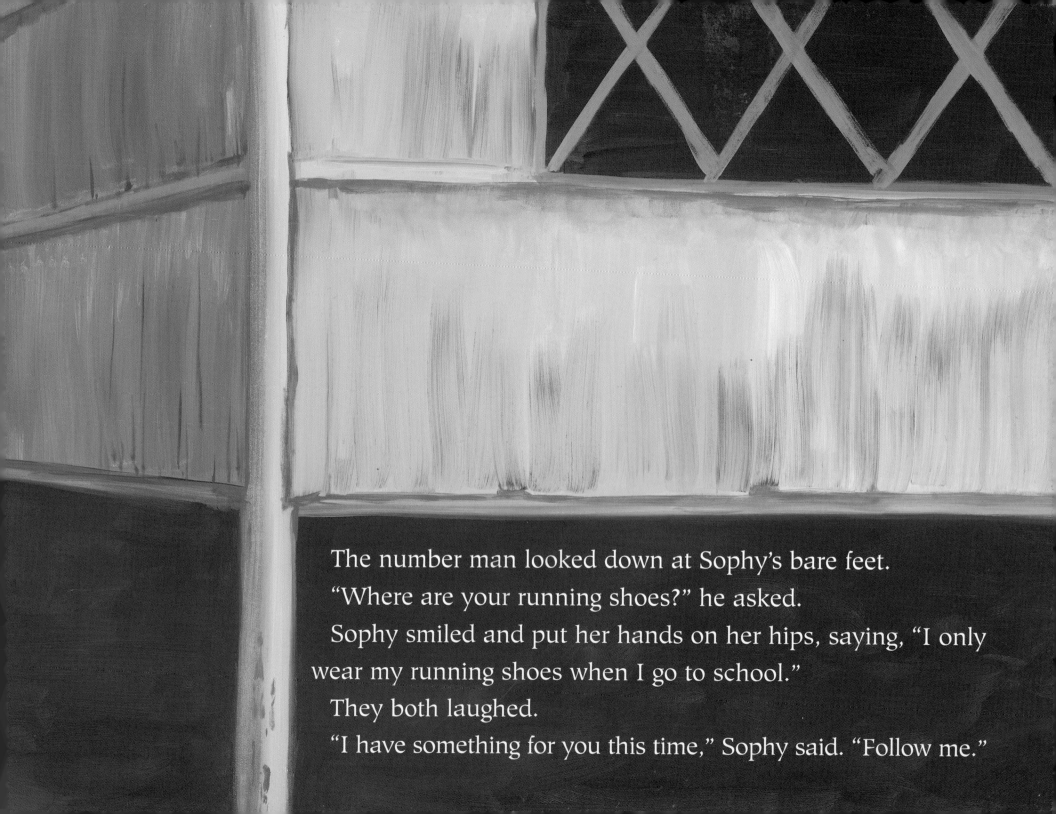

The number man looked down at Sophy's bare feet.

"Where are your running shoes?" he asked.

Sophy smiled and put her hands on her hips, saying, "I only wear my running shoes when I go to school."

They both laughed.

"I have something for you this time," Sophy said. "Follow me."